FOOTWEAR

FOOTWEAR

A Short History
of
European and American Shoes

BY

IRIS BROOKE

Theatre Arts Books
NEW YORK

Library of Congress Catalog Card Number 79-109116

Part of this book was originally published by St. Giles Publishing Co. Ltd., London, in 1949 under the title *A History of English Footwear*. Grateful acknowledgment is made to them.

Published by Theatre Arts Books
333 Sixth Avenue / New York, New York 10014

Printed in the United States of America

CONTENTS

FOOTWEAR

INTRODUCTION

*" This person being highly blamed by his friends, who
demanded,—was she not chaste? was she not fair?—
holding out his shoe, asked them whether it was not new,
and well-made. Yet, added he, none of you can tell where
it pinches me."*

Plutarch (circa 100 A.D.) *relating the story of a Roman
being divorced from his wife.*

IT is impossible to estimate at what phase in
development on this earth, man first thought of
shielding his feet from the natural hazards of
climate and conditions. We may assume, of
course, that Adam stubbed his toes on leaving the
garden of Eden when all good things came to an
end and he was no longer protected from the pains
and tricks of an unfeeling world; then with the killing
of the first beast, he fashioned some form of foot
covering from the skin of his kill.

Or if we consider it from the scientific point of
view, when the evolution of man reached the biped
stage, the unfair division of weight to the hind legs
necessitated some covering to protect them from wear
and tear. Certainly the earliest caveman drawings
give indication of some form of foot covering.

1

Our modern knowledge of ancient history, from the scientific side, boggles at dates and data earlier than about 4,500 years B.C. We do know, however, that the valley of the Nile nursed an advanced civilisation at approximately 4,000 B.C., a civilisation that thrived on art and beauty, whose upper classes at least, were elegantly clothed and finely shod. Their sandals were primarily designed to protect the soles of the feet from the heat of the desert sands. A few straps arranged with skill and care gave the foot freedom and cool comfort with a minimum of friction or pressure. The earliest examples of such sandals can be seen on the feet of Egyptian statues, now in the British Museum.

There are also many actual examples of sandals—which have been discovered during recent years in the Egyptian tombs, these include a pair of calf-leather sandals from the tomb of Tut-ankh-amen, which are now in the Cairo Museum. These sandals have a flexible sole about a quarter of an inch thick, with a strap coming up between the big toe and the second, which was held in place by a wide strap from either side of the heel to the instep. This can be seen on the foot of the statue of Memephthah, now in the British Museum. Other examples of the Egyptian sandal vary little from this adequate design. There are, however, one or two pictorial records that show a turned-up toe to the sandal with sharp point, and these appear to be more solid in their construction.

Introduction

The common sandal of ancient Egypt had a sole made from plaited papyrus, woven into a mat of varying degrees of thickness, similar to those still worn in many parts of the world to-day. Such a sole was reasonably hard wearing and comparatively simple to make, but had nothing of the wearing capacity of leather. See Fig. c below.

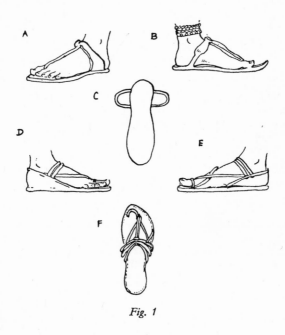

Fig. 1

The drawings above are examples of the known types of Egyptian and Assyrian sandals, A, B, and c being Egyptian, D and E ancient Assyrian and F, a modern example still worn in similar districts to-day.

3

From the bas-reliefs which exist, recording the history and doings of the Assyrians and Babylonians, we can see that their soldiers were equipped with boots and leggings, an advancement on the sandal, probably suited to the long marches over rough ground that the warlike Assyrians found necessary evils in their conquering programmes. Other pictorial tablets of the Tigris-Euphrates civilisation show the curved-toed shoe of the Hittite, dating from about 1,000 B.C. Such turned-up toes are probably the earliest examples of a fashion that might well be the forerunner of the Moorish slipper, the Dutch clog and the cracowes of the 15th Century. Certainly whenever a hard sole has been used, the obvious toe protection was a curved point.

At various phases in the history of footwear, practically every available substance has been employed for their composition or decoration, but persistently through all other fashions or crazes, the leather shoe, sandal or boot, seems to have predominated. The Assyrians also wore a particularly interesting type of sandal with a heel protection (see Figs. 1 D and E), the sandal was attached from the heel side by a thong that was wrapped around the big toe. I have given both the inside and outside of the foot in the accompanying diagram, to show how this interesting arrangement worked. From contemporary drawings it looks as if there were a ring attached to the shoe through which the big toe was thrust.

Introduction

The earliest records of footwear in colder climates are probably the Chinese and, as far as we can estimate, they were wearing felt boots, or fur-lined leather ones, from the time of their earliest civilisations in the Tang dynasty. Thick-soled sandals were also worn as far back as modern knowledge can penetrate, presumably in the hotter climates of China. The slipper of felt, silk or rush which covered the deformed foot of the Chinese woman was a miniature replica of those worn in the privacy of the household by her lord and master. Whilst the footwear of China and Japan has always remained round-toed, the Indian and Persian races have always favoured the curved and pointed toe; the latter style percolated throughout the South East of Europe and along the Mediterranean coasts of Africa sometime during the spread of the Mohammedan religion, and probably inspired the Crusaders at a later date to introduce this fashion in moderated or exaggerated form into our country. Extremes of heat and cold would seem to be the obvious reasons for footwear, rather than wear and tear, and the lighter the colour of the skin, presumably the softer the foot, for few of the negroid races have found it necessary to adopt any form of covering for the feet.

It is but a short step from the Egyptian to the Greek civilisation or from the Greek to the Roman, so that it was only natural that sandals should still be favoured in these comfortable climates, but what is of some considerable interest is that the warlike

5

Romans again adopted the same type of boot for their legionaries as the Assyrian hordes had worn in the days of Nineveh. Similar boots were worn by the Greeks when hunting, as shown below.

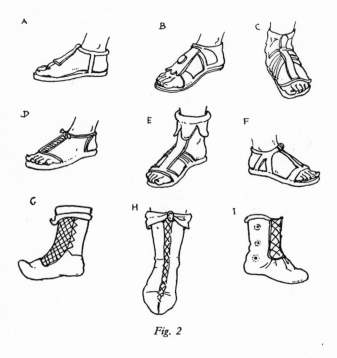

Fig. 2

Fig. 2 G shows the Assyrian version, 2 H Roman and 2 I Greek. Other examples on this page are Greek and Roman sandals.

The Romans attached a considerable amount of importance to uniforms, thus red leather shoes were reserved for senators only, and shoes of black leather were worn by patricians.

Rome's gradual expansion throughout Europe during the first centuries A.D. embraced such fashions of the countries of their occupation that appeared suitable and sufficiently refined for a ruling nation. During this steady absorbtion period, the Romans swept into Britain, which was, according to Greek records, already fully aware of the treatment and use of leather. Britain was to the Romans one of their wealthiest conquests and the rich supply of metals and leather did much to enhance its value in their desire for weapons, armour and other exportable commodities. Curiously enough, on the withdrawal of their legionaries, the art of making metal armour seems to have been totally lost for several centuries, but that of tanning, though slow and tedious, seems to have survived without any noticeable lapse.

When Rome ceased to be a power in Southern Europe, the invading Goths and Huns scorned the elegant sandal of the conquered decadent race and brought their coarse leather footwear, designed primarily for a colder, rougher climate, into general use. The Norsemen and Vikings were becoming a formidable power in Northern Europe soon after the fall of Rome. They found skins warmer and more practical than the silks and linens of the Southern races, and fur-lined boots and woollen leggings a more adequate protection from snow and ice.

7

At this particular stage in the history of mankind the idea of socks and stockings, as we know them, had not been devised or had ceased with an earlier civilisation, but the practice of wearing a leg covering from ankle to knee or thigh was generally accepted and such coverings whether in wool or skin were tied to the leg with leather thongs criss-crossed to hold them closely and give added warmth. There was nothing comparable in such primitive footwear, with the sophisticated gilded boots and sandals of the earlier civilisations, but utility governed the clothing of the early centuries A.D. and every man was his own cobbler, as every woman spun and wove the household clothing.

To reconstruct a picture of Britain before the Norman Conquest, it is necessary to remember that a hundred fashions had been incorporated into a comparatively small population. Much of the Roman teaching must have been retained even while Scandinavians, Danes, Saxons and Celts all claimed their camps and settled in this country. Many styles of footwear must have been in use at the same time from the dyed leather shoe of the Roman official to the raw-hide mocassin-type worn by the peasants. Legend deals romantically with the lady's gilded sandal, while such pictorial records that exist, show side by side, the jewelled and decorated shoe and the simple dark leather slipper with pointed toe.

Our claim to the use of leather dates from very early times and in the first century A.D., we find

leather mentioned as a main export from these
islands. There seems little doubt that the art of
successful tanning was one of Britain's earliest crafts
and probably under the Roman occupation the more
delicate features of leathercraft were given considerable encouragement both for home use and export
purposes.

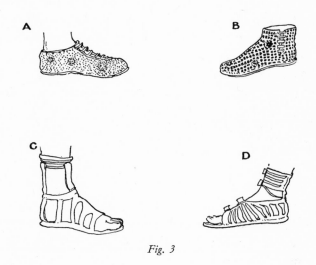

Fig. 3

Examples of Roman-British footwear such as
those in Fig. 3 that are still in existence, show a
considerable skill and high degree of finish, but here
again it is difficult, if not impossible, to find out if
such footwear was brought into Britain from Rome,
or if it were actually made in this country. Such
footwear that was introduced into Britain by the

Romans would in all probability be the first sandal to be seen on these shores, but even before the Roman occupation, British tanners were considered competent craftsmen.

It seems, therefore, reasonable to suppose that if fine examples of leather work were to be seen and handled here, the imitative instinct of the leather worker would undoubtedly have provoked him to produce similar, if not identical, specimens, in a craft that he was admittedly a master.

The general state of poverty and scattered leaderless communities to which the country was reduced on the withdrawal of the Roman legionaries, resulted in a series of raids and incursions which left the harassed population little time to practise any of the gentler crafts, self-preservation from complete slavery or extinction, being the primary motives of life.

In the ensuing years such communities gathered together under the leadership of an appointed king and built themselves a stronghold against the ruthless invaders and established a certain degree of comfort for themselves inside a fortified wall.

Country towns and villages made their own footwear on traditional lines in the most serviceable fashion then known to them. Shoemakers working for the more extravagant-minded portion of the population devised their own particular schemes of decoration or extravaganza, but until the middle of the thirteenth century when the elongated toe was first introduced by the

Crusaders, the main features of footwear consisted of a soft soled shoe with a foot-fitting upper, the toe slightly pointed so that the shoe could be worn on either foot.

Leather always has been a beautiful surface for designs, stamping, embossing or engraving, and we can easily imagine when looking at the finely worked shoes on ancient tombs that this art was carried out with considerable care, and when required, the most delicate and intricate cut-out effects could be carried out without fear of breakage or tearing. Colour also within certain limitations could be introduced, and apparently the insertion of precious stones and gold and silver filigree work. It will be noticed that with such finely wrought shoes, there are always plain bands left where the shoe takes the greater part of the strain. Such bands were obviously left so that there would be less likelihood of the shoe breaking away.

CHAPTER I

THE conquest of Britain in 1066 brought foreign fashions into a country that must have been comparatively wild and desolate, and according to Norman standards, somewhat uncivilised. Although the Saxon kingdoms in England retained a court life that favoured a degree of elegance and wealth that would surprise us to-day, these courts were isolated high-spots frequently many days' journey apart, where life was carried on in security and comfort behind a fortified wall with adequate services to be had and skilled craftsmen to add dignity and elegance to the secluded life of these fortunate individuals. Outside these walls, however, the peasant population, who were engaged in agricultural pursuits, lived a hard and dangerous life, continually on the watch for the bandits and vagabonds that descended from time to time on the scattered homesteads, killing and stealing anything worth the trouble. These people in all probability, were still going bare foot in summer and roughly shod with only partially dressed leather in winter.

Fig. 4.—1150

Such hides that they managed to keep for their own use were needed for a variety of purposes other than foot-wear such as water-bottles, purses, belts, bags, coats and jerkins as well as harness for the oxen which seem to have entirely supplanted the horse during this era.

The Norman conquerors, for a great part, were the superfluous or adventurous aristocracy of a civilised country. Their foot-wear and clothing was of a considerably superior quality to that of the Anglo-Saxon. The Normans favoured a pointed toe and further embellished their foot-wear with bands of decoration, the same simple geometrical design similar to those we can see to-day around a Norman doorway or arch. These bands of embroideries or stamped leather were worn in a variety of ways : across the foot from toe to instep, around the ankle or across the bend of the toes. Their shoes to our modern eye were not particularly hard-wearing for the sole was as pliable as the upper and was indeed, frequently all part of the same hide or skin. None of these shoes are still in existence, but there are numerous contemporary drawings and a few effigies and brasses that can be studied : amongst these is the famous Bayeux tapestry which was probably finished during the twelfth century and shows clearly the general tendencies, if not the actual detail, of Norman footwear. It seems reasonable to suppose, that in many cases, the bands of decoration were sewn on to strengthen a seam in the shoes, or give added support to ankle or instep, rather than from entirely decorative motives. A variety of fastenings were employed, but the split instep with an

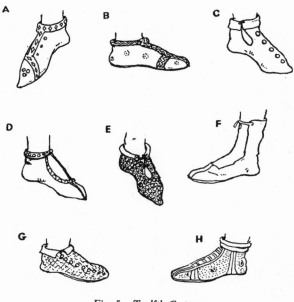

Fig. 5.—Twelfth Century

ankle fastening at the top seems to have been the most general. Laces and buttons were used both at the side of the shoe and up the instep, in much the same way as they are to-day. Short boots reaching

15

only a few inches up the leg, and also laced, or cut sufficiently loose to pull on without a fastening,

Fig. 6.—1130

were sometimes worn and a few contemporary drawings show a long soft leather boot reaching

almost to the knee, the top decorated with embroideries. These types of footwear persisted with little modification for nearly two hundred years. Variations appear on the following pages, but it is almost impossible to say definitely that any of these styles went out of date for at least a century after their first appearance.

Probably the earliest reference to the shoe-making craft in England occurs in Archbishop Alfric's colloquy written during the eleventh century. In his dialogue with the shoe-wright, the shoe-wright says : " I buy hides and skins and I prepare them by my craft and I make of them boots of varying kinds, ankle leathers, shoes, leather hose, bottles, bridle thongs . . ." This useful list gives us a complete inventory of the footwear of the eleventh century. Boots of varying kinds, ankle-leathers which were the protective covering worn by simple folk and leather hose, the footless leg covering which was worn over the braes or trousers.

There seems to be little evidence of the cordwainers' guild existing much before the end of the thirteenth century, though in the year 1272, a variety of fines and prosecutions were imposed on leather workers making boots and shoes from inferior quality sheep-skin. Obviously, the guild must have been working for some time and, moreover, was both proud and jealous of guarding their quality and rights. Cordwainers were the shoe and boot-makers and their name was taken from the fine hard-wearing goat-skins peculiar to

Cordova in Spain, which for many centuries were imported into this country for the makers of good shoes. From such early records, we may find that the composition of " bazin " or sheep-skin and cordwain was prohibited except when the former was used for the upper part of a long boot. No bazin worker was permitted to use cordwain and no cordwainer was permitted to use bazin.

Cobblers were not in those days the menders of shoes that we know them to-day, they were a recognised and specialised trade that bought up old shoes and re-made them for re-sale. The amount of new cordwain that they were permitted to buy was limited by the guild. There were other controls in force, also imposed by the craftsmen concerned, and aimed at the protection and preservation of the high standard of their Guild-work.

It is difficult to describe the shoes of the middle ages, for though contemporary drawings are full of a variety of shapes and designs which give us a very good idea of what people's feet looked like at a distance, it is almost impossible to say definitely how they were cut, from what materials the detail and decoration were made, or how the apparent precious stones and metals were introduced into the surface of the leather. In the effigies of these figures, the shoes appear to have very flexible soles though the uppers are nearly always raised, ribbed and decorated above the surface.

In all probability, the highly-decorated and extravagant shoes of the wealthy were taken to pieces so that

Fig. 7.—1230

the decorations might be used again ; such decorations were probably much sought-after by the cobblers of that time.

Historical records and anecdotes as well as the colourful illuminations of the twelfth and thirteenth centuries give us to understand that shoes and boots were dyed all sorts of colours, including gold and silver, though only traces of colour remain on the existing shoes. We are told that Henry II in 1189 had a pair of green leather shoes decorated with bands of gold to which his spurs were attached with strips of red leather.

Soon after the first Crusade, oriental styles in design and footwear took a strong hold on the imagination of the English public. Long-toed shoes quickly became a popular extravagance that continued in favour and fashion for nearly two centuries. Some of the early examples are particularly interesting—in Fig. 8 is a shoe with a fish-tail toe. Even the women indulged in this strange fashion which must have been amazingly uncomfortable and difficult to manipulate.

A feature of the thirteenth century was an interest in knots and imitation knots where material was drawn through a ring. An example of this can be seen on page 13 (Fig. 4), where the soft leather at the top of a boot is pulled through a small ring, so that the top fits the leg. Any superfluous material in a garment was, at this date, treated in a similar manner. These fashions were not, as far as we know, repeated at any later date, and are typical of a few years only at the end of the thirteenth century. Though pointed and elongated toes were first worn at the turn of the

Fig. 8.—1260

thirteenth-fourteenth century, the truly absurd exaggeration of this fashion was not seen for more than a century later. The early examples fitted the foot fairly closely to the toe when the shoe tapered

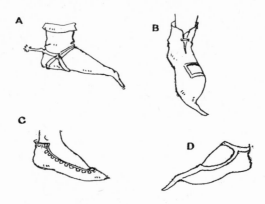

Fig. 9.—*Thirteenth Century*

into a narrow point to match the liri-pipe at the point of the hood. This point was not very long, only two or at most four inches beyond the toe and cut so that it turned away to the outside even though it commenced at the big toe. This presumably saved the wearer from treading on his own toes as he walked. (Fig. 9 b).

Matthew Paris gives us some delightful drawings which show us how the shoe looked in the middle of the thirteenth century, and a rich variety of designs in footwear occur in the Bible Moralise which is approximately of the same date. What is extremely difficult to understand is just what they were made from and in many cases how they were fastened. The ankle fitting boot with the rolled top which occurs so frequently in drawings of the twelfth and thirteenth centuries, and is apparently lined with contrasting material, never appears to have any method of fastening, though obviously it must have had to fit in the manner suggested (see Fig. 9 A). The majority of these shoes were fastened with a button, particularly those with an open instep (Fig. 9 D), and one or two examples show us a shoe buttoned from toe to ankle.

CHAPTER II

His rode was reed, his eyen greye as goos ;
With Powles window corven on his shoes
In hoses rede he went fetisly.
Y-clad he was full smal and proprely.
                    Miller's Tale—1380.
                    Geoffrey Chaucer.

A FRESÇO in St. Stephen's Chapel, Westminster, shows us an excellent example of a pair of shoes, probably similar to those Chaucer mentions the Parish Clerk wearing in his " Miller's Tale," " Paul's window craven on his shoes." (See Fig. 10 A.) This fresco was painted during the reign of Edward III and gives us a clear indication of the design and pattern favoured by the wealthy during the early fourteenth century.

The window referred to by Chaucer was the rose window in old St. Paul's. This was similar in design to that which is in the front of Notre Dame in Paris, and the intricate traceries of the window lent themselves well in the design that might fill a circle.

Chaucer's delightful and colourful pictures of the characters that appear in his *Canterbury Pilgrims* gives

A

C

B

Fig. 10.—1370

us intimate details of dress and manners of the late fourteenth century. The following extracts from his poem tell us a great deal about footwear in his age.

In the " Miller's Tale," his description of Alison tells us that her shoes or boots were laced.

> " Hir shoes were laced on her legges hye ;
> She was a prymerole . . . (Primrose.)

The Wife of Bath well-equipped for her journey was wearing new shoes and scarlet stockings.

> " Hir hosen weren of fyn scarlet reed,
> Ful streite y-teyd, and shoos ful moiste and newe
> Bold was hir face, and fair, and reed of hewe."

In the enchanting description of the golden-haired Knight, Sir Thopas, we find a reference to Cordwayne, the gentleman's shoe leather of that time :

> " His heer, his berd was lyk saffroun,
> That to his girdel raughte adoun ;
> His Shoon of Cordewane.
> Of Brugges were his hosen broun,
> His robe was of ciclatoun,
> That coste many a jane."

The Monk wore " supple " boots and the Merchant also, obviously clad in the fashionable attire of his calling :

> " A Marchant was ther with a forked berd,
> In mottelee, and hye on horse he sat,
> Up-on his heed a Flaundrish bever hat ;
> His botes clasped fair and fetishly . . ."

Edward III to Henry VII—1327-1485

In many ways, the fourteenth century marked a revolutionary step in the development of this country. England had become England, and was no longer a nation of serfs governed by " foreigners." The wool trade was beginning to bring wealth into the homes of farmer and peasant alike, and the general standard of living was very much on the upgrade. Wool and leather were within the reach of all, and fashions, once the prerogative of the few, became the amusement of the many.

Probably the Hundred Years War did much to delay the progress of the countryside, but a gradual lightening of the load, and a desire for intellectual stimulus as well as improvement in craftsmanship, is discernible throughout the fourteenth and fifteenth centuries.

By 1381, Chaucer is laughing at the fashion of his countrymen, whilst William Langland in his *Creed of Piers Plowman* (*circa* 1360), points out the still unfair persecution of the peasant in contrast to the wealth of the Church. The ploughman, pitiful and poverty-stricken, is described in the following manner :

His cote was of a cloute
That cary was y-called ;
His hod was ful of holes,
And his heare oute ;
With his knoppede shon
Clouted ful thykke ;
His ton toteden out,

27

As he the lond tredede ;
His hosen over-hongen his hokshynes
On everich a syde,
Al beslomered in fen
As he the plow folwede.

In modern language :

His coat was patched
And of coarse cloth,
His hood was full of holes
And his hair out,
With his knobbed (or nailed) shoes
Patched very thickly,
His toes peeped out
As the land he trod,
His hose over-hung his shins,
On all sides.

A pair of fourteenth and early fifteenth century shoes with " knoppede " soles are illustrated in Fig. 11 A and B, taken from a shoe recently excavated. The heel has a heavy iron rim or crescent and the soles are studded with nails. This example has curiously enough a tie front, a fashion that did not occur again until the end of the sixteenth century.

Again in the same poem, the comparison drawn between the original monks of the Franciscan Order and those of Piers' time, tells us that " buckled " shoes were worn :

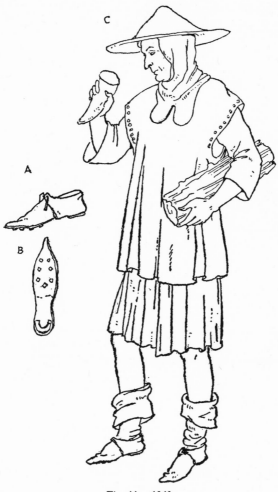

Fig. 11.—1340

" Fraunceys bad his brethren
　Bar-fot to wenden ;
　Now han they buclede shone,
　For blenyng in harde weder
　Y-hamled by the ancle . . ."

Unfortunately we have no clear knowledge of what these " buclede shone " were though presumably the reference would be the fastenings which might have been buttons.

In *The Vision of Piers Ploughman* :

" Proude preestes coome with hym
　Mo than a thousand,
　In paltokes and *pyked shoes*."

Piked-shoes were a curious feature of the fourteenth century, gradually becoming more and more exaggerated, until the long-pointed toes peculiar to the early years of the fifteenth century were made so long that they had to be tied up to the knee.

It is interesting to learn that both a " souter " and a souteresse " are mentioned in *Piers Plowman*. A souter was a shoemaker and a " souteresse " was a female shoemaker.

Shoes were made from coloured leathers and the wealthy indulged their fancy not only in long " piked " toes, but in brightly-coloured footwear, often stamped with designs in gold or contrasting colours. Leather was not always used ; velvet and other rich and brilliant materials were employed and cloth of gold could be used by lords. The cutting-out of intricate

Fig. 12.—1440

designs and " tooling " the leathers gave to the shoe an ornamental interest seldom achieved in the shoes of a later date.

The general method of fastening the shoe was by a lacing on the outside of the foot (see Fig. 13 B), but the flimsier and more " elegant " shoes of the early part of the century were often buttoned at the side in much the same manner as a child's shoe is to-day. The fashions of the early years of the fourteenth century were particularly insistent on buttons as an ornament as well as serving a useful purpose. Cutting the edge of all garments into leaf shapes or points was also a fashion that found its way on to the upper edge of boot or shoe.

The fifteenth century was undoubtedly a century of excesses, and shoes were notably one of the most extravagant absurdities of the time. The wealthy were struggling hard to maintain their *status quo*, and tried with diminishing success to bar the rising middle classes from interfering with their prerogatives in fashionable absurdities. In the year 1420, a law was passed barring the wearing of long " piked " shoes by any person whose income did not exceed £40 per annum. A prince, however, might be permitted to wear his two and a half feet long if he cared to.

The absurd lengths to which these pointed toes were carried can be imagined when we realise that they were often chained to the knee and silver bells attached. The old nursery rhyme of :—

" Ride a cock horse to Banbury Cross,
    To see a fine lady ride on a white horse,
    With rings on her fingers and bells on her toes,
    She shall have music where ever she goes."

is taken from this fashion. However, the chained

IRIS BROOKE

shoe proved tiresome as well as dangerous, and was soon abandoned for a less awkward length. The shoes peculiar to the mid-fifteenth century seem to

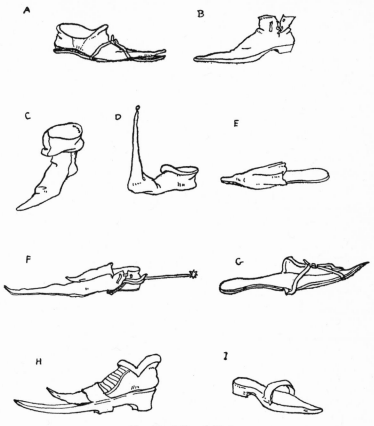

Fig. 13.—Fifteenth Century

have all been very much the same. Figs. 13 A and 13 E are both taken from excavated examples, and the interesting method of attaching the long spurs—

sometimes as long as the toe of the shoe—can be clearly seen in Fig. 13 F.

"Pattens" or clogs were worn over the shoes— Fig. 13 G and Fig. 13 H are contrasting examples, the fact that the toe is extended in each case almost to the end of the " pike " is an interesting feature. The reason must have been that of fashion alone, for it seems improbable that these lengthy " clogs " could have been anything but supremely uncomfortable and difficult to manage.

Wooden soles were quite frequently worn on the shoes of the early fifteenth century ; a hinged wooden "patten" can be seen in Salisbury museum and is interesting in that it has metal support at the heel, when the majority of " pattens " were attached at the toe only.

It is a little difficult at this particular stage to find out if contemporary references to pattens actually mean shoes or pattens. Among the interesting letters of the Paston family, there is one written by Edmund Paston to his brother John in 1471, asking him to purchase for the family various items of clothes, this request includes the following :—

" iij dozen poyntes wytte red and yellow price vjd. iij peyers of pateyns (pattens) i pray you let Wylliam Mylsant purvey for them. I was wont to pay but ijd ob for a payer, but I pray you let them not be lefte behying thou' I pay mor : they must be lowe pateyns ; let them be long enow and brode upon the hele . . ." Here we are confronted with the possibility that

Edmund meant shoes, as it seems improbable that he would wish to buy three pairs of pattens at a time, or

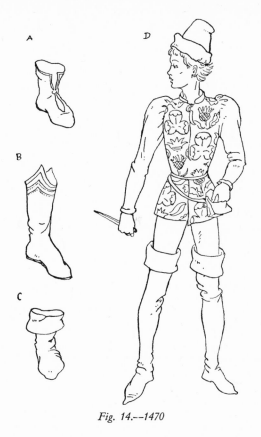

Fig. 14.--1470

that it was necessary to send to a special " purveyor " for a patten. However, the reference to " let them be low pattens " might conceivably be to the flat leather sole rather than the wooden supported one illustrated.

Long leather boots were worn, reaching to the thigh, and in some cases, these were actually tied to the waist ; usually they were lined with some contrasting

Fig. 15.—1490

colour. Hose with a leather sole were also quite popular. It is almost impossible to see clearly from contemporary drawings how these hose were devised, but in all probability they were cut on the cross from some fairly "stretchy" material and the leather sole sewn on afterwards.

As late as 1468, the excesses of the "piked" shoe were calling forth a barrage of abuses, so much so that the Pope was appealed to intervene. As a result a "bull" was issued against the cordwainers and cursed those who made any long "pikes" past 11 inches in length. This "bull" was proclaimed at St. Paul's Cross, but history does not state if the curse ever took effect, or if it had any effect whatsoever on the cordwainer's work. It was not, however, more than about fifteen to twenty years later that this curious fashion disappeared altogether and was almost immediately replaced by an excess in the opposite direction, the width of the toe and not the length.

It is interesting to contrast the existing drawings of the excessively long-toed shoes, the few actual examples that are still to be seen in various collections, and the very modest "pikes" to be found on effigies and tombs of the period. What might easily have been considered "artist's licence" in the long whip-like extension, was apparently quite a normal contemporary feature, otherwise there would not have been the laws and the Pope's bull expostulating against their use. We must, therefore, assume that in spite of no real shoe existing to-day of the exaggerated type, they were an all too common occurrence.

Women of the fifteenth century did not follow the absurd fashions in shoes ; though their toes were long and pointed, the point was never more than an inch or two beyond the shoe for the obvious reason that at this time the skirts were fantastically long and had to be bunched up in front to take even the smallest step unless the wearer wanted to find herself inextricably entangled in the voluminous folds of her gown. As walking was a slow and tedious process—what with the unwieldy head-dresses and the many yards of trailing gown—the ladies probably wore shoes made from materials other than leather; for any journey out-of-doors was made on horseback.

CHAPTER III

We will not leave one lord, one gentleman:
Spare none but such as go in clouted shoon;
For they are thrifty honest men and such
As would, but that they dare not, take our parts.

Henry VI, part II.
Shakespeare.

THE main features of the Tudor shoe, though to our eye appearing neither practical nor comfortable, outlasted the dynasty. This feature was slashing the leather so that a coloured lining might be arranged to show through the cuts and attract the eye.

Shoes worn in the time of Henry VII and VIII were square-toed, and cut so low at the sides that it is difficult to imagine how they ever stayed on the foot, let alone protected it. Many of them had no heel at all, a narrow strip of leather half an inch high as seen in Fig. 17 b, was the only support at the side of the foot and in many examples this " mule " was not even tied round the instep to secure it to the foot.

39

Shown on this page is an example of a lady's shoe. The drawing of the figure is taken from one of Hans

Fig. 16.—1520

Holbein's delightful records of an English woman (*circa* 1520.) The shoe shown in Figure A is obviously similar and comes from a collection of shoes found during excavations in London.

The Tudors—1485-1602

The toe gradually became more and more duck-billed in shape till it stood out some inches from the actual foot. Sometimes even eight or nine inches in width, see page 17. This fashion reached its extremity about the time Henry VIII died and during Edward VI's reign. In Mary's reign, the shoe retreated to a reasonable shape and gave the heel a certain amount of protection once again.

The widening of the toe was a fashion which Mary eventually put a stop to by a declaration that the width of the toe must not exceed 6 inches, surely wide enough to be a nuisance to the wearer, but apparently not wide enough for the extravagant-minded.

It would seem probable that knowing the Queen's addiction to the Queen of Hearts in Alice in Wonderland's favourite speech " Off with their heads," that for once this decree was given some attention. Normally the history of clothes does not appear to have been in any way affected by the regulations that have been imposed on fashions from time to time. There are dozens of these royal and clerical gestures recorded in existing proclamations but we do not see the obvious or expected abandonment of the particular excess in question. The same fashion appears in contemporary portraiture in exaggerated or diminishing form for many years after it is supposed to have been put aside.

There are a considerable number of these squared-toed " slippers " still in existence and these can be examined in detail. Where the slashes in the upper appear in a row, a seam has been made just below to

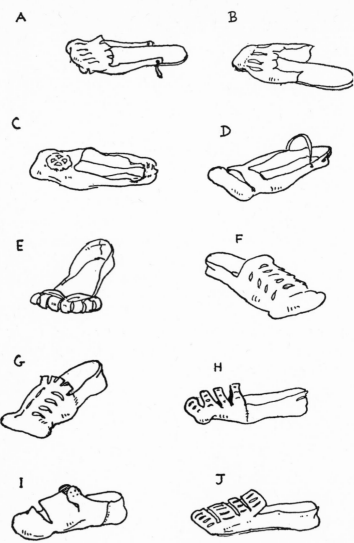

Fig. 17.—1500-1550

stop the cuts from tearing further than fashion demanded. The leather in all cases is black with age and oil
which has been used to protect it from damp and
depreciation. Children's shoes follow the prescribed
styles in every detail, the square rolled toe is just as
exaggerated in these minute examples as in those of
the adult.

Why such an uncomfortable and apparently ineffec-
tual foot-covering should have remained fashionable
for half a century or more is one of those queries lost in
the mists of obscurity. We may assume that pedes-
trianism as we know it now did not exist, but it would
still seem improbable that every short journey was
made on horseback, or that even the necessity to cross
the village street was not hampered unduly by a flap-
ping sole and a shoe that did little or nothing to
protect the foot from mud and filth.

In *Ralph Roister Doister* by Nicholas Udall which
was written probably about 1550 or even earlier, the
following lines occur :

> . . . " And though your teeth be gone, both so
> sharp and so fine.
> Yet your tongue can run on pattens as well as
> mine."

Obviously this is a contemporary allusion to the
clattering sound that was normal in the streets of the
mid-sixteenth century from wooden-soled pattens.
Unfortunately there are no actual examples of pattens

existing that could reasonably have been worn over the light and flexible sole already described in this section, although there are a considerable selection of both fifteenth and seventeenth century examples.

Boots were worn for riding—a soft leather boot with intricate piecing so that it fitted closely at the back of the ankle to hold a spur. (Figs. 19 A and 19 B). Women when riding had their voluminous skirts thrust snugly into a " bag " in the same manner that they had done for a century and a half.

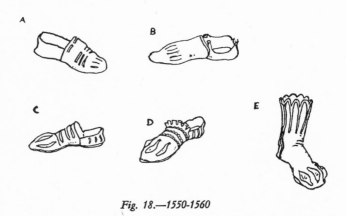

Fig. 18.—1550-1560

Spanish fashions were adopted in England during the few years that Philip endured the English climate and tolerated Mary's moods and manners. When he returned to Spain the extravagances and fantasies of the Spanish courtiers remained in vogue and Elizabeth, new from her imprisonment, and her ladies, indulged in an orgy of fashionable excesses.

44

The Spanish shoe was foot-fitting and though still slashed and decorated, it was to all appearances a comfortable fitting slipper, see Figs. 18 B, C and D.

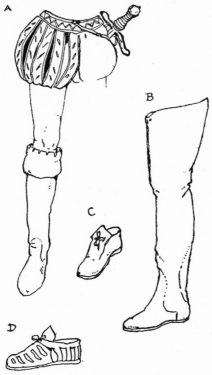

Fig. 19.—1580

The front of the shoe came well up over the instep and to enable the wearer to put it on or take it off without undue strain, the sides were often cut down to the sole so that the heel could be pulled back. (See Fig. 18 B).

45

Fig. 20.—1560

The Tudors—1485-1602

Still flat soled, such shoes were made of leather dyed a variety of colours, white being particularly fashionable. The Spanish fashion for black and gold was never pursued with any obvious fervour in this country. Where previously the slashings had been devised so that the lining might be pulled out in little bubbles and puffs of colour, now the lining only showed when the foot was bent as a series of bright and contrasting lines.

Sometime between the seventies and eighties the first high heel made its appearance midst cries of derision and satirical rhymes and jingles. Such heels were as popular with men as they were with the fairer sex, and though they were indeed " high " after the flat sole of previous ages, existing portraits would not give us to believe they were more than an inch and a half in height. One such portrait of Henry III of France was, and may be again in the Louvre, and shows a heel that might possibly have been two inches high. Apparently these heels took some time to get used to, and many a swollen calf and sprained ankle was the immediate result. Both cork and wood were used for the heel and later, metal and leather in layers were employed. It was probably some years after their introduction that the appropriate position was decided upon for the heel that would give the foot support as well as the much coveted " elegance." Certainly during the next two centuries every conceivable type and shape of heel was tried out for the benefit of both sexes before it eventually became an entirely feminine feature.

At about the same time a strange fashion in footwear which emanated from Venice was that of wearing "chopines" (see Figs. 21 and 22). These odd-looking stilt-soles were made of cork, the top furnished with a slipper toe so that the foot could be accommodated, the solid base sometimes being cut out in much the same way as a hoof. Contemporary comments and records tell us that ladies could not walk alone in them unless supported on both sides. Apparently, however absurd though the fashion was, it remained in vogue for some twenty years and proved a not altogether unsuccessful method of negotiating the filthy streets without damage to the cumbersome and unwieldy farthingale. The elegant ladies of the 1590's found themselves satirized on all sides :—

"Tired with pinned ruffles, fans and partlet-strips
With busks and vertingales about their hips,
They tread on corked stilts at pris'nors pace
And make their napkin for their spitting place."

So runs a contemporary reference to the ladies of fashion.

Clogs or "pattens" had been worn throughout the century to lift the foot from direct contact with the mud and filth of the village street, but these had never been adopted generally by any but the peasant class, and the fantastic idea of ladies adopting and exaggerating such a fashion called forth more than normal comment and abuse. Shakespeare mentions them in *Hamlet*, Act II, Scene ii, when Hamlet remarks the players' change of height when dressed for the

Fig. 21.—1602

performance of the "Murder of Gonzago" :—
"By 't Lady, your ladyship is nearer to Heaven
than when I saw you last, by the altitude of a
chopine."

As late as 1645, John Evelyn, visiting Venice, gives
us the following amusing description of ladies endeavouring to manipulate these clumsy contrivances :
" . . . it was now Ascension Week, and the great mart,
or fair, of the whole year was kept, everybody at
liberty and jolly ; the noblemen stalking with their
ladies on choppines. These are high-heeled shoes,
particularly affected by these proud dames, or, as
some say, invented to keep them at home, it being
very difficult to walk with them ; when, one being
asked how he liked the Venetian dames, replied, they
were mezzo carne, mezzo legno, half flesh, half wood,
and he would have none of them. . . . Thus attired, they
set their hands on the heads of two matron-like
servants, or old women, to support them, who are
mumbling their beads. It is ridiculous to see how these
ladies crawl in and out of gondolas, by reason of their
choppines and what dwarfs they appear, when taken
down from their wooden scaffolds ; of these I saw
near 30 together, stalking half as high again as the rest
of the world. For courtesans, or the citizens may not
wear chopines . . ."

I have inserted this interesting anecdote in this
chapter rather than in the seventeenth century because
it would seem to be the only visual record of a fashion
which had come and gone in England some thirty or

forty years earlier. The actual contemporary records are more in the nature of a satire than an accurate description.

The extravagances in dress generally which were adopted during the later years of Elizabeth's reign led to an incredibly lavish display of jewels and precious metals. This unexampled and ostentatious splendour spread literally from top to toe. Contemporary portraiture shows us a bewildering array of pearls, emeralds, rubies, diamonds and other gew-gaws worth apparent fortunes, sewn or clipped to every item of clothing worn by both man and woman. In two portraits of Elizabeth, her shoes are decorated with gigantic stones worth a king's ransom, one of these pairs of shoes appear to be made from gold kid or cloth of gold, the other, white satin. Both have soles about half an inch or more in thickness. These were probably cork rather than leather, the toe is neither pointed nor square, but slightly rounded.

Some diversity of opinion exists as to the actual authenticity of the fabulous-looking ornaments found in contemporary portraiture. How much was really the property of the owner and how much artist's licence, it is impossible to prove. We may safely assume, however, that royal portraits at least were decorated with some adherence to actuality.

Boots when worn at all, were entirely for hunting, fighting and riding, and few examples are still in existence. On page 45 is an example of a long riding-boot of 1580. Others show signs of having been slashed in the contemporary fashion. The Duke of Altta's boots (Fig. 18 E) are a single example of a short decorated ankle boot.

It was during the last decade of the sixteenth century that the shoe was first tied with a " latchet "— a fashion that when once established existed with little variation for over two hundred years. The front or vamp of the shoe was cut long, coming up well over the instep ; two flaps, one from either side of the foot were tied with a leather thong over the vamp of the shoe leaving an opening at the sides (see Fig. 22 c). These shoes had very thick soles, frequently made from cork, and an early example of a wedge sole can be seen in diagram 22 D.

It must have been several years before the turn of the century that the idea of fixing a rose or rosette over the tie of the shoe first became popular. In Shakespeare's *Romeo and Juliet*, Act II, Scene iv, Romeo's quip, " Why, then is my pump well flowered," would give one that impression. It is also from the same play that we learn of a special type of shoe being worn for dancing :—

Mercutio. "Nay, gentle Romeo, we must have you dance."

Romeo. " Not I believe me : you have dancing shoes with nimble soles : I have a soul of lead, so stakes me to the ground I cannot move."

The flower or rosette decoration was universally worn during the early years of seventeenth century, but this Shakespearian reference would undoubtedly be several years earlier than one would expect, for *Romeo and Juliet* was written soon after 1592.

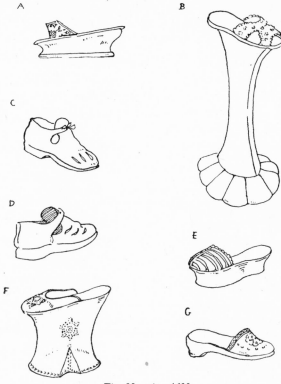

Fig. 22.—*circa 1600*

The above drawings of chopines are all taken from existing examples to be found in various museums throughout this country. Their dates vary slightly, but they are probably more typical of the early seventeenth century than the late sixteenth.

CHAPTER IV

" Her feet beneath her petticoat,
Like little mice, stole in and out,
As if they feared the light."
　　　　　　John Suckling.　1637.
　　　　　　A Ballad upon a Wedding.

ONE of the most interesting existing specimens of English leather craftsmanship of the early seventeenth century is a pair of boots made for Charles I when he was about seven or eight years of age and still the little Duke of Albany.　At this time Charles was suffering from rickets and some fears as to whether he would ever be able to walk without irons on his legs had been allayed by the assistance of an enterprising bootmaker who introduced brass supports into the heel and ankle of the boot.　The work is finely executed, the boots are not unduly heavy, yet they must have given a reasonable support to the child's weak ankles.　The heel about an inch high is hollow, and a leather spring or pad has been arranged so that the metal edge would not jar the royal wearer as he walked. These boots on minute examination give one the impression that they had been worn only for riding. There is little sign of wear on the sole though the uppers are slightly rubbed and show the form of the foot. It may have been due to this early deformity of Charles I that boots became so amazingly popular during his reign. Most contemporary portraits show the king wearing boots which he probably found more to his taste and vanity than the rosetted shoes of his time which accentuated the thinness of their owner's legs.

During James I's reign, the heel which had caused trouble and derision during the last few years of Elizabeth's time, was quite generally accepted and became a necessary part of the shoe rather than a fantastic addition. Such heels were now made from several layers of leather, and the shoe peculiar to the first quarter of the seventeenth century, was apparently a comfortable and well-cut arrangement which differed only in its ornamentation, a rosette or a bunch of ribbons or lace which could cost a small fortune. In Henry Peacham's *The Truth of our Times* (1638), the price of these lace rosettes and other shoe ornaments varied from 30/- to £5, and as the £1 of that time was worth at least 6 or 7 times its value to-day, there would appear to be some truth in the puritanical accusation that a shoe ornament cost as much as a man's suit.

The rosette was not always worn by women at this time, probably their petticoats did much to hinder the foot without the added trouble of a rosette which might not even be seen.

Fig. 23.—1630

Robert Herrick in his *Delight in Disorder* does, however, mention the shoe-string :

> . . . " A winning wave (deserving note)
> In the tempestuous petticoat ;
> A careless shoe-string in whose tie
> I see a wild civility.
> Do more bewitch me, than when Art
> Is too precise in every part."

56

Fig. 24.—1630

When men wore shoes after 1625, the " boot hose " or over-stocking was also worn. This was tied at the knee and fell down the leg in layers of lacy frill giving the effect of a boot without the discomfort.

A peculiar feature which first appeared in France about 1620 was the extension of a sole under the heel (see Fig. 24 A and B). In some of the drawings of the time this appears to be a separate " chopine " or oversole, whilst in others the sole actually continues in one piece from toe to heel and remains on the ground when the wearer has lifted his heel from the ground. This oddity is best explained by the accompanying drawings. There must have been considerable difficulty in mounting a horse in a hurry.

Feet quite suddenly during the Thirties became a feature for fantastic decoration, and the so-called bucket-topped boots of the cavalier vied in exuberant and lavish display with the curled and frizzed hair and feathered hats so dear to the hearts of theatrical costumiers. These boots were cut in all manner of shapes, as can be seen in the accompanying drawings. Their incredible size and clumsy appearance was at once exaggerated and emphasized by the wearing of " boot-hose." Boot-hose were finely embroidered or laced stockings with exaggerated width at the top so that they might fall elegantly over the top of the boot and add to the general atmosphere of disordered extravagance which was the fashion of the time. The clumsy jack-boot of the Cromwellian armies was in marked contrast to the absurdities of the cavalier.

IRIS BROOKE

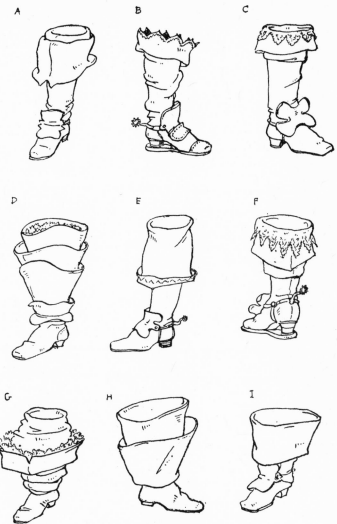

Fig. 25.—*Mid-Seventeenth Century*

Walking was almost impossible in the really fashionable boot, and in some of the amusing drawings by Abraham Bosse, the gentlemen appear curiously bow-legged and ungainly. In France particularly, was this fashion carried to excess and when Cinq-Mars, Louis XIII's favourite, was beheaded in 1642, he left behind him three hundred pairs of lace-trimmed boot-hose. It is difficult to imagine, to-day, how anyone could have found a use for so many apparently useless furbelowes, but boots were worn in the drawing-room at this time and were not considered anything but the necessary decoration for a man of fashion.

In the year 1660, Louis XIV was presented with a pair of shoes with broad vamps and high red heels, the insteps decorated with bows sixteen inches in width, the ends decorated with smaller bows with rosette centres. This strange fashion was immediately adopted and replaced the previous boot in favour. The high red heel became general and the majority of existing Restoration shoes still show signs of this peculiarity. (See Fig. 27).

On January 22nd, 1660, Samuel Pepys makes an entry in his famous Diary, " This day I began to put on buckles to my shoes." By this comparatively simple entry, we know positively that the fashion for buckles on shoes in preference to the tie must have come in just before the ribbon bows, it was probably temporarily eclipsed by the absurdities of Louis XIV's court fashions, to which I have just referred and came in again to stay for over a century. What is so

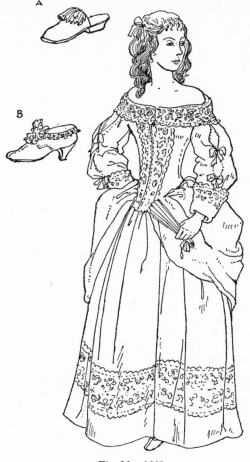

Fig. 26.—1665

particularly interesting about this remark is that it completely explodes the theory that the Puritans of the Commonwealth wore buckles on their shoes instead of

61

the lacy rosettes and bows of ribbon adopted by the Royalist Party. We know by Pepys' remark, " This is

Fig. 27.—1665

the first time that ever I wore buckles on my shoes," that until 1660, his shoes had been fastened by latchets. Bunyan during his imprisonment kept his family from starvation by fixing metal tags on to the leather shoe-laces worn by everyone at that time. Bunyan's first imprisonment corresponds with the date when Samuel Pepys first wore buckles.

Two days after this reference to buckles, Pepys makes another entry of interest, " I took my wife to Mr. Pierce's, she in her way being exceedingly troubled with a pair of new pattens and I vexed to go so slow it being late." Probably Elizabeth Pepys' pattens were similar to those worn about 1680, though obviously not so well-cut or she would have not experienced quite so much trouble on her short walk. It can be well imagined that nothing could be more uncomfortable than a patten which did not fit the shoe over which it was worn. The fashion which became more prevalent during the eighteenth century for making a pair of pattens especially to fit each pair of shoes, shows us that the craft was carried out with considerable care and efficiency.

It was at about this date that women's feet first began to be a noticable feature of attractive interest, and a variety of elegantly embroidered silk, satin and velvet shoes with high heels and a long vamp or tongue made their appearance from beneath the tucked-up petticoats. Such shoes were square-toed (see Fig. 28 B and C), and the fastening was, particularly in the Seventies and Eighties, under the tongue ; later the tongue was arranged under the fastening and led to the buckle becoming the main feature of the shoe of the eighteenth century.

The extravagance of the Restoration period and the latter years of the seventeenth century ran in the direction of imported luxuries rather than the products of

Fig. 28.—1688

the homeland. Oriental silks and satins, French and Brussels lace, Spanish velvets and fine leathers were all

employed in the costly manufacture of shoes. Mary
Evelyn writes in her *Mundus Milebrus* (1690) amongst
a long list of requisites for the trousseau :—
" Four cushion-cloths are scare enough
Of point and Flanders, nor forget,
Slippers embroidered on velvet . . ."
The pointed toe first appeared in the Parisian
fashion-plates of 1680 by Bonnart, and as the majority
of our fashions came from France, there is little doubt
that this was approximately the date when the small
point first replaced the flat square one. But the new
emphasis on a differently-shaped foot did not, for the
first time in the known history of footwear, extend to
masculine fashions. The pointed toe was an entirely
feminine fashion for a quarter of a century or more, and
the exaggerated high heel in conjunction with the
pointed toe assisted considerably in the fashionable
deception that women of quality had tiny feet.

As the century drew to a close, the heel on the men's
shoes became higher and higher until in some instances
it was about $4\frac{1}{2}$ to 5 inches in height (Fig. 29). The
shape of these heels was still on the heavy side, but
the fashion of having a heel sloping outwards as
worn on the boots had completely disappeared on
shoes. The long tongue was also exaggerated until
it reached some inches up the leg, well above the
ankle where the top was rolled over to show a
contrasting lining, either scarlet to match the heel of
the shoe or some other obvious contrast. The top
of the tongue was often scalloped or cut out in a

Fig. 29.—1690

Fig. 30.—1700

pattern and the buckles which fastened the two sides across the instep became larger and more ornate in design, until sometimes they were wider than the foot itself.

After half a century of fanciful and decorative footwear for men, it is something of a shock to find that the jack-boot of the time of William III was such a clumsy affair as existing specimens now show us. The examples on the previous page were all made a few years before the close of the seventeenth century and all have a singularly thick sole and clumsy heel. The various ways the spurs have been fastened is of particular interest, the strap and chain under the instep were both used and it will be noticed that the spur, though it differs in shape in each example, is supported by a metal strut from the back of the heel which is actually attached to the boot. The flap which covered and protected the front of the foot from the rub of the stirrup, is still as it was fifty years earlier on the bucket-top boot, but the whole delicate craftsmanship of the 1640's has completely disappeared in the heavy jack-boot of the nineties and the years immediately following 1700.

CHAPTER V

" Let firm well-hammer'd soles protect thy feet,
Tho' freezing snows, and rains, and soaking sleet
Should the big last extend the shoe too wide,
Each stone will wrench the unwary step aside ;
The sudden turn may stretch the swelling vein
The cracking joint unhinge, or ankle sprain
And when too short the modish shoes are worn,
You'll judge the seasons by your shooting corn."

                John Gay." Trivia."
                    1715.

THERE has been for many years a general tendency to separate the Georgian era from the Stuart with an almost impenetrable line of definition, but actually when the Hanoverian dynasty began there was no such obvious change of fashions and manners.

England under William and Mary had become accustomed to foreign manners—Queen Anne's husband though one hears so little of him was Danish, and introduced many European manners into the court life of the day. Fashion throughout these years looked for guidance from the Courts of France and almost in defiance of the cruder northern habits claimed affinity with the fantasy and extravagance of Louis XIV and XV.

The somewhat heavy and overwhelming solidity, attributed to Dutch influence, which we find in the jack-boot described in the last chapter (which, however, remained in general use for the soldier) very quickly gave way to the studied negligence of a softer long boot for riding, and as skirts grew fuller—the skirts of men's coats as well as the hoops in ladies' petticoats—an elegant ankle became a matter of importance to man and woman alike. Indeed, the hooped skirt actually showed the ankle for the first time and made it doubly necessary for attention to be lavished on hose and footwear simultaneously.

It was here, then, during the first quarter of the eighteenth century that buckles—at first a fastening—became primarily an ornament. Imagination and extravagance ran riot in the choice of these baubles. Fortunes were lavished on them and stones and precious metals, once considered a dress ornament found their way on to the instep of a shoe.

The history of shoe buckles is an extremely interesting one, and from small and useful beginnings one can trace their varied career through a century and a quarter, until finally brought to a halt by the classic revival of the Regency period.

The most extravagant excesses in the buckles of the eighteenth century were carried out in the French court and their hasty exit from French fashions in the nineties was in all probability due to the largest and most magnificent specimen being called " Artois " buckles, christened after the Comte d'Artois, younger brother of Louis XVI whose delight in fashionable excesses even rivalled Marie Antoinette's.

Although the really ostentatious specimens of buckles were to be seen in the glittering splendour of Versailles, many of these same gigantic gew-gaws were manufactured in this country. Birmingham, the seat of industry even in the eighteenth century, carried out on a very grand scale the manufacture of shoe buckles. Records show us that some 2,500,000 buckles were produced in this town annually and a vast number of people were kept busily engaged in their manufacture. Prices of buckles ranged from 1/- per pair to 20 guineas, and every conceivable substance was employed to give variety to these costly baubles.

Unfortunately for Birmingham, Dame Fashion is no respecter of Industry, and in 1791, when classic fashions were beginning to sweep the cumbersome farthingales and wigs off the streets and out of the drawing-rooms, buckles were deemed old-fashioned and declassé and the sandal-shoe became the rage. In vain did Birmingham buckle-magnates endeavour to struggle against the tide of fashion, and a petition was made to the Prince of Wales, demonstrating their pitiful plight, and revealing the shocking fact that some 20,000 persons were now out of employment and starving in the streets of Birmingham, all because nobody wanted buckles any more. The Prince, duly shocked, did his best to assist by continuing to wear buckles himself, but the fashion had spent itself and a once flourishing industry died.

The assumption, however, that all eighteenth century shoes had buckles is incorrect. Many ladies'

Fig. 31.—1720

shoes were tied in much the same manner as a laced shoe is to-day, though the " latchets " were narrower and usually only had one eyelet each side for the ribbon tie. (See Figs. 31 and 32).

George I to Victoria—1714-1837

Ladies' shoes during the eighteenth century passed from experiments in high heels to every type of heel

Fig. 32.—1740

with the exception of the wedge. In one point only did they adhere to any formula and that was that the heel, however curved or high began well under the instep sweeping down in a curve and giving full support to the foot. This feature can be seen clearly in the drawings on the opposite page, which have been specially selected for this purpose. The inside of the high heel itself was never straight. Because of this the pattens, now reduced to a sole with a support, which were generally worn at this time, were all curved to fit well under the foot and give a solid support which did not slip once the latchets were tied over the instep of the shoe. Ladies' shoes were normally made from fabric, and finely embroidered, usually the patten was made from the same material, and many of these still remain in our museums in an amazingly good state of preservation. There are singularly few examples in leather. The heel was often, though not always, covered with the same material as the shoe. Shoes were all lined and the edges were bound.

It was during the first quarter of the eighteenth century that the fashion for decorating the heel of the shoe caught the fancy of the extravagant and romantic-minded. Rhymes and jingles were written on the heel, jewels were set in the pattern, and the ever-popular heart motif was introduced not only on the heel itself (see Fig. 33 B), but traced on the leather under the instep. This pretty conceit was normally applied to bride's shoes.

During this time, men's heels gradually became lower and lower until about 1740 when they all

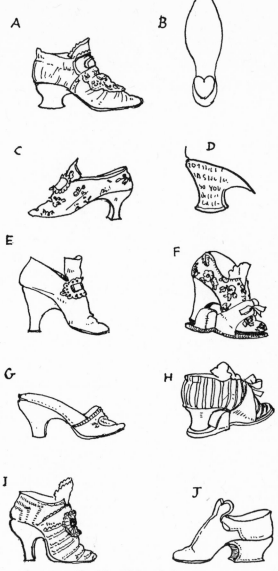

Fig. 33.—*Eighteenth Century*

Fig. 34.—1740

appear to have been about three-quarters of an inch to an inch in height. The high heel seems to have had some subtle connection with the high wig for as this absurdity collapsed into the neat tie-back powdered affair, so heels also descended, and when, in the Seventies, the wig once more started to climb into the piled and pomaded edifice treasured by the " macaronis " of that age, so also did the heel once more rush up to the precipitous height of six inches, both of which fashions, however, lasted only a few years if that. (See Fig. 35).

The making of men's shoes had, during the early years of the eighteenth century, reached a very high standard in fine craftsmanship. They were both well-cut and beautifully sewn. Existing examples show us that the handwork is so fine that it seems impossible that they could have been made without a machine. The design seems to be very similar in all examples, the buckle being the only method of fastening the shoe. The heel is wide and low, similar to those found most convenient by men of to-day. (Fig. 34 A and B).

Many of the shoes shown in this chapter were probably originally adorned with a buckle, but such buckles have since found their way into collections or else been utilised as ornaments in a different capacity. Fig. 33 I is taken from one of the many examples now in the Museum at Salisbury and shows a buckle of finely-cut crystal set in silver. This shoe was given to a Mrs. Powell, of Hurdcote, by Frederick, Prince of Wales, in 1740, and is made from scarlet embroidered brocade ; the heel is about two and a half inches in height.

A   B

Fig. 35.—1775

Fig. 36.—1794

It is interesting to ponder at this stage on the strange habit of " toasting " a lady with wine poured into her shoe, for such shoes are typical of those worn in the most extravagant period of the century, without even a leather lining to stop the wine pouring out as soon as poured in.

So flimsy were women's shoes at this time that George II had to supply his daughters with a new pair of shoes once a week, at the cost of 6/- per pair. This was no royal extravagance for, in the accompanying documents of dress allowances, twelve pairs of thread stockings had to last each princess for two years.

As the century advanced, heels became even higher, and by about 1775, we find examples with heels actually six inches in height (see Page 78, Fig. 35 A and B). Fig. A is said to be a man's shoe, and it will be noticed that the back line of the heel is almost straight. The inside is still curved. This example has a six-inch heel.

Ladies' shoes were similar in design until the 1790's when the French Revolution literally took the stuffing out of French fashions and simplicity was carried to a fantastic imitation of the classic.

The flat " pump " with ribbon ties over the instep supplanted the heeled shoe, and remained in fashion for some 40 years in England. For many years, however, the older woman clung to her high heels, flat shoes were essentially for the young as also were the clinging and practically transparent dresses. Rowlandson gives us many lively contemporary

Fig. 37.—1795

caricatures that show the two styles side by side as late as 1820.

Fig. 38.—1795

During the Napoleonic Wars, fashions generally assumed a military air and boots which had only been worn by soldiers and for riding for half a century or more, once again came into fashionable prominence. The Wellington boot and the Blucher

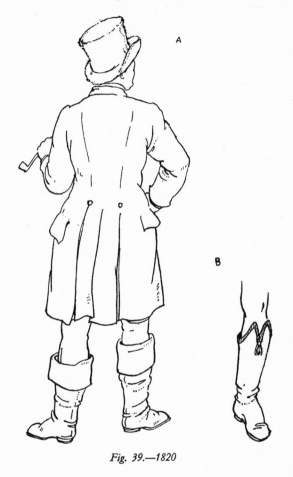

Fig. 39.—1820

boot, both taking their names from their military namesakes, were so popular that the excuse of riding was not necessary for their use. They were worn when promenading and even dancing, and an elegant caricature of a loose ankle boot was not considered out of place in the drawing-room. Such boots were often decorated with tassels or lined with contrasting leather and turned down at the top. See Fig. 38.

The English squire of the late eighteenth and early nineteenth century appears to have lived in his boots rather to the astonishment of French visitors. Such boots had a turned-down top, lined with a yellowish-buff, and hundreds of contemporary drawings and caricatures show us how very popular they were.

Philip, Duke of Orleans, endeavouring to make a good impression in England, wore boots of this type, and it is from this style of boot that John Bull first established his traditional form of footwear.

An example of these boots can be seen on Fig. 39 A. In Fig. B, on the same page, is an example of another style of boot that became almost as popular. This was called the Hessian boot and it was generally worn with a tassel hanging down the cut in the front.

It is a strange contrast that at this time when women were wearing a sandal of the flimsiest, men were everywhere stalking about in boots.

For formal occasions, a low-heeled pump was worn ; this usually had a flat buckle on the toe, but was cut low in much the same fashion as those worn by the women.

About 1810, the boot was adopted by fashionable ladies for general wear. These were flat-soled with an extra layer or so of leather under the heel. The uppers

were sometimes made from coloured leather and
sometimes partly leather and partly material.   They

A   B   C

D

Fig. 40.—1810

were fastened on the *inside* ankle with lacings (see
Fig. 40 D).   A few years later the fashion for boots was

even extended to dress occasions, and brides' boots and dancing boots both made their début. An

Fig. 41.—*1825*

amusing pair of white satin boots with large mother-of-pearl buckles on the instep, and lace frills, has elastic sides covered with gathered lace, and a heel about three-quarters of an inch in height. These can

Fig. 42.—1830

be seen in the Blackmore and Wilts. Museum at Salisbury, and are dated 1825 (see Fig. 41 B). Several pairs of coloured morocco boots appear in the same collection, all with elastic sides.

87

During this time, a new kind of clog or chopine was used for country wear with a metal hoop attached to the wooden or leather sole to lift the wearer well off the ground (see Fig. 40 A and B).

Although the flat sole was generally worn by women during the 1820's and 30's, there are many examples of a small heel, never high, but enough to give a little support to those who found the flat sole too tiring. We must remember, however, that walking for ladies was at this time almost unknown! The carriage was a necessary equipment, and gentle exercise was carried out, if at all, in the ornate gardens so popular during the early years of the nineteenth century.

Existing shoes show us that feet were, on the whole, very small, and that such shoes were not made to stand up to anything rougher than a paved or tiled promenade. Heavier types no longer exist, probably they were literally worn out, and the flimsy examples now to be seen were kept either for sentimental reasons or because they were too fragile to wear very often.

HOW
70s →

IRIS BROOKE.

CHAPTER VI

" What profits now to understand
The merits of a spotless shirt
A dapper boot—a little hand—
If half the little soul is dirt."

—*" Punch," Feb.,* 1846.
Alfred, Lord Tennyson.

LTHOUGH a patent was taken out in 1790
for a sewing machine to stitch leather, the
early attempts to do so were far from
successful and it was not until the 1850's that a
sewing machine was actually used for shoemaking.
A riveting machine was, however, introduced during
the twenties, but though this increased the number
of shoes and boots that could be produced—and
lowered their price—it was still a far cry to the
perfection of a machine-made shoe. Shoes had
to be " broken-in " by their wearer and the resulting
corns and dislocated toe-joints would give us the
impression that it was the feet that suffered the
breaking-in rather than the shoes.

The early years of Victoria's reign were coincident
with the Industrial Revolution, consequently we find
the rather ugly and, to our minds, tasteless trends
in shoes and boots that were a peculiar feature of
early Victorianism.

Footwear

The forties, fifties and sixties favoured the boot with a cloth top; this fashion was equally popular with men and women and an amusing variety of tops appear in the contemporary fashion plates. Plaid and striped materials were quite as popular as a plain colour; elastic sides vied in popularity with button fastenings. Leather was used for the toes and heels and both kid and patent leather were in great demand.

Evening shoes for women were usually made from satin coloured to match the dress. Regulations in dress were somewhat rigid, especially for the young girl, as Victorian etiquette demanded that youth must be dressed only in white for evening occasions. Black and white satin or kid pumps were the only correct wear for the young girl throughout the crinoline period. The young matron, however, was entitled to please her husband by wearing pale colours even if she was still in her teens, but only the middle-aged and eccentric were to be found wearing any really colourful dresses—or shoes—at night.

Children were expected to wear boots for most occasions, though the flat sandal slipper with crossed ribbon tie was often worn by little girls during the summer months.

Women's feet were not supposed to show under the voluminous hoops and petticoats of the crinoline, and if they did they had to be small. To this end, the smallest possible shoe or boot that could be jammed on to the foot was encouraged by mothers

Fig. 43.—1840

Fig. 44.—1842

of young daughters in much the same way as the
" waist " was forced into being. Contemporary

Fig. 45.—1865

drawings of young ladies of fashion of the sixties
show an ugly bulge above the tightly-buttoned boot
which obviously was no exaggeration of the facts

of the time. This singularly unattractive phenomenon was much exaggerated by the wearing of striped stockings, as shown on page 93.

During this same period men's footwear was, for the most part, only boots. Walking boots, riding boots, dress boots (with plaid or striped tops) and even evening boots of shiny patent leather, though evening shoes were still worn usually for dancing. Buttons, laces and elastic sides were all approved methods of fastening such boots. Buttons, flat mother-of-pearl ones like shirt buttons, were the most fashionable as the foot appeared more elegantly shod than in the easier elastic-sided affairs which soon looked shabby and sloppy, for elastic has a tendency to get slack and stand away from the ankle in a most unbecoming manner.

The carpet slipper, the embroidered or tapestry one and a hand-painted velvet slipper all made their appearance during the early years of Victoria's reign and became a fittingly sentimental gesture on the part of young ladies who wished to show their men folk how well they could sew or paint.

As the century progressed towards the seventies the crinoline subsided into the soft and jiggling waves of the bustle and the toe at least was visible once again. The flat heel had given place to a tiny, curved one, and the toe was elegantly finished in a sharp and rather uncomfortable-looking point. When from about '79 to '82 the skirts lifted from the ground and showed the ankle the high heel and the high boot appear to have been generally worn even by children.

We must remember, however, that most of the fashion plates and many of the drawings of this time

Fig. 46.—1885

were copied from the French styles, for this was a time when France was very much the leader of fashion.

95

The exaggerated little heel, the pointed toe and the high cloth-topped boot with elegant embroideries and minute detail decoration were a considered luxury; the general tendencies in English footwear were not, if we can judge from drawings and photographs, either dainty or elegant, though possibly they were hard-wearing, a quality for which English footwear has been renowned for some considerable time.

Children at this time were seldom permitted the comfort of shoes except indoors; the favourite type of indoor shoe for the smaller child being those worn by " Alice " in Tenniels' charming drawings of " Alice in Wonderland," a patent leather shoe with an ankle strap. Little boys, except when dressed in velvets and lace of " Little Lord Fauntleroy "— when they also wore patent leather shoes with buckles —were always to be heard clattering around in sensible boots often tipped with iron "blakeys." The tags with which to pull them on stood out from behind, making them look even more uncouth than necessary.

Sport for women as well as men had an effect on footwear about this time. Tennis and bicycling became very fashionable during the Nineties. A rubber-soled shoe with canvas or buckskin top and banded with black or brown leather was introduced for tennis and boating. Boots, of course, were worn for skating.

Spats were a great favourite with the well-dressed man. They could be either white, grey or black. For sports, such as shooting and fishing, a gaiter was worn, not very long, but rather like a long spat, only leather. These were worn with knickerbockers and stockings and are an outstanding feature in all the contemporary "sporting" drawings and illustrations, particularly in *Punch*.

The cloth-top boot was a necessary feature for all dress occasions; these usually had grey cloth tops. Another variation of the spat was a short "collar" which could be worn round the ankle. This was not more than a couple of inches deep, and had two or perhaps three buttons.

Curious though it may seem to us to-day, the fashion for boots almost amounted to an obsession during the last quarter of the century. Rudyard Kipling sums up the horrors of war in his famous poem "Boots" (1893).

"Don't, don't, don't, don't, don't look at what's in
front of you,
Boots, boots, boots, boots, moving up and down
again,
Men, men, men, men, men go mad with watchin' 'em,
And there's no discharge in war."

Although this cannot be considered as anything except a war story, the theme was one which could easily be applied to the boot mania of the late Victorian era.

It was in the mid-nineties that footwear manufacturers in England suddenly realised that the Victorian tradition of good, dull ideas was coming

Fig. 47.—1900

to an end. America was producing a far smarter shoe at a considerably cheaper price and English women were only too pleased to welcome the new fashions. For many years the wealthy woman had been buying her shoes and boots from Paris, but the prices were so high that this "luxury trade" was too limited for it to have seriously affected the English manufacturer. Now, however, his position was threatened by the importation of thousands of cheap and attractive shoes, their quality was certainly not comparable with English workmanship, but the low price and interesting variety in styles did more than compensate their durability.

Obviously new designs and ideas had to be devised to battle with this unexpected competition, and almost immediately the boot disappeared for "smart" wear and the shoe, no longer a mere kid slipper, took its place.

Glacé kid and bronze slippers decorated with a small ornament on the toe had for many years been the only possible shoe that could be worn for dressy occasions ; now, however, coloured shoes were once again fashionable for evening wear, and with such shoes stockings of the same colour might be worn.

During this time the brown shoe first made its appearance and with the brown shoe, brown stockings, a daring departure from a convention more than half a century old. Men also found the brown shoe or boot more convenient for country wear and black was reserved for town and dress occasions.

Women's shoes could be laced or buttoned at the sides and it was not long before the strap across the instep found popularity for both indoor and outdoor shoes.

We must realise that in all probability the worthy boot had remained in fashion so long because of the general Victorian sentiment of the age that decried " glamour " in any form as a possible inducement to immorality. Shoes were worn by " theatrical " people and the " arty " section of the community and were therefore " not nice."

A word might be said here of this same " arty " section and their new attitude to footwear. Under the guidance of Ruskin and his followers, a considerable portion of the so-called " intellectual " female population had shed their bustles and boots and appeared in public in sandals and flowing gowns preaching the return to the simple life and home craftsmanship. Probably their sandals were the product of local craftsmen, though advertisements appear in contemporary papers which would give one to understand that someone was manufacturing them !

IRIS BROOKE

CHAPTER VII

I hold the very strongest views
About elastic-sided shoes,
While made-up ties and 'dickeys' too
Are both of them, of course, taboo!
    —" Dressing."
     Harry Graham—1924.

THOUGH the American shoe had been welcomed with enthusiasm by the fair sex, the Englishman would have none of them and the English shoemaker was quick to seize upon this loyalty and make further efforts to please the conventional male. Men's shoes, soon after the turn of the century, took on a new vitality. The brown brogue and the sports shoe in tan and white—rudely referred to as the " co-respondent's " shoe—all appeared for the first time and their solid workmanship and durability did much to enhance them not only in English eyes but throughout Europe.

For normal city and town wear, black shoes with spats were general but the black boot still vied in popularity with the shoe for at least the first decade of the century.

Fig. 48.—1907

The Edwardian era was one to which we all look back in surprise that it should have ever existed in this chaotic century. Tradition was everything, and

102

in the matter of footwear such tradition established in the previous century was obviously not to be

Fig. 49.—1911

sneered at. The Naughty Nineties had loosened the laces of the boots, but not the corsets. Dignity must be upheld in the all-important matter of colour schemes and deportment. Black, tan, beige, grey and white were all nice colours for ladies' shoes, the pointed toe and the Louis heel were both correct for formal and dress occasions.

Sports, however, were claiming the attention of the younger generation, and rubber-soled shoes and brown brogues were as much a part of a young lady's equipment as the neat Oxford shoe for walking and the strap shoe for indoor wear.

Children still wore boots until about 1908, when the shoe quite definitely supplanted them in popularity. Children's gaiters in leather or felt were worn from about this time too, reaching up to or above the knee and being buttoned on the outside. The fashion for gaiters for women first appeared when the ankle began to show. In a *Punch* of 1912, a small boy is depicted staring at a lady's gaiter-clad legs, and underneath is written: " I suppose you're the Bishop's wife." Apparently the fashion was new enough then to cause comment.

The shortage of man-power and the success of the Suffragette Movement, stimulated the Women's Services into being soon after the 1914 War began. Solid and sensibly flat-heeled shoes and boots soon took the place of the high-heeled walking shoe of a decade earlier.

The Russian boot for women first appeared in England during the war years.

The long-laced boot similar to those worn by police-women today was worn both in town and

Fig. 50.—1915

country during the war years but vanished within a very few years of 1918.

Convention and restriction generally were strained to breaking point if not completely defied in the early years of the Twenties, and much that had been considered the very root and essence of life was gaily abandoned in a mad desire to express a new-found freedom. Pre-war standards of living and dressing were obsolete, and women, no longer fettered by the colour rulings of black, white, tan and dove-grey which had been the entire spectrum of colour in walking shoes pre-war, were only too eager to adopt the new skins and coloured leathers that shoe manufacturers were pressing on to the market.

Legs had, during the war, appeared under the shortened skirts of the women in uniform, and this fashion once established gradually became more and more exaggerated until the whole art of being " smart " and dashing was focused on the legs and feet. Light coloured stockings, at first beige, grey and pink, were worn in the Twenties to emphasise the shoe. By 1923, when the Duke and Duchess of York were married, the Duchess had in her trousseau a considerable number of coloured shoes : this gave a stimulus to the already growing fashion, and also opened a way to further experiments in ladies' footwear. Scarlet, blue and green were the first colours used for dying leather, but within a very short space of time light blue and violet, yellow and

a variety of other shades appeared on the market.
The heel which had for practical reasons become
fairly low during the war was still fashionable,

Fig. 51.—1927

though the toe was pointed. Court shoes were worn
with high heels, strap shoes with either a cuban
heel of about 1½ inches or a highish curved one

were both equally popular. About this time the fashion which, for several centuries had been dormant, introducing cut outs into shoe uppers, reappeared and quickly became very popular. The strap shoe was first to be cut in this manner and designs of simple geometrical symbols were cut both on the toe and on the sides of the strap. From this " cutting-out " style was developed the sandal shoe, though several stages of cutting away resulted before the sandal straps were cut down to a bare minimum in the early Thirties.

Sports shoes of the Twenties still followed the traditional design of an " Oxford " shoe and were laced over the instep; some of these were brogued and had a welted sole for country wear, whilst others were cut in much the same manner but with a medium cuban heel. Suede was becoming increasingly popular for both men's and women's shoes, and such shoes were often " trimmed " or banded with calf.

Odd though it now appears, when during the early Twenties, the skirt dropped suddenly to the ankles, the heel of the shoe also dropped and we find the hideous fashion-plates of those unfortunate years depicting unlovely flat-footed figures with a waist-line almost round their knees and pudding basin hats well down on their eyes. Stockings were of light colours and seemed to accentuate the size of the foot when so little ankle was visible. Fortunately this fashion lasted only a very short

A

B

C

D

"CHUNP AWAY
AT THE
STONE "

Fig. 52.—1931

109

time and when the leg was once more exposed the shoe immediately became of primary importance.

The flat heel or very low heel was undeniably popular during the later years of the Twenties though a very high heel was also favoured by the more sophisticated. The difficulties of dancing the Charleston and Black-Bottom were well nigh insuperable in a very high heel so that evening shoes were made of a sandal type with low heels. Gold and silver kid were very much worn and a variety of coloured fabric shoes, crepe-de-chine, satin, velvet and lame made often to match the dress were also very popular.

The low heel, having once come into fashion, was such a favourite with many that it has never really gone out again. By the beginning of the Thirties, a rich variety of shoe styles were to be had in every shoe shop, heels high or low, pumps, sandals, slippers, ankle-strap, instep-strap, sling-back, buckles and laces in a dozen different colours and types of leather.

Experiments in the treating of animal and reptile skins had resulted in the production of fine soft leathers which could be worn comfortably; the first lizard and crocodile shoes used were not soft enough to be really comfortable but by the late Twenties or early Thirties, they had reached a stage of pliability which adequately served the purpose.

Men's shoes during these years, also, developed a new freedom both in design and the leathers used. Sandals and light-weight sports shoes both took

their places; these were also made in a variety of
leathers and suede was a particular favourite during
the Thirties.

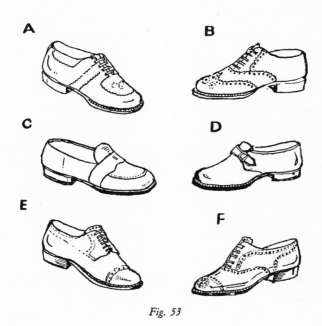

Fig. 53

The above drawings are examples of the newest
styles of men's footwear fashionable in the years
immediately preceding the war.

Fig. 53 c is a popular slipper type which avoids
the necessity of lacing.

Fig. 54.—1945

In the drawings shown on this page, we can see clearly how old styles have been adapted and turned into something new and suitable for modern needs.

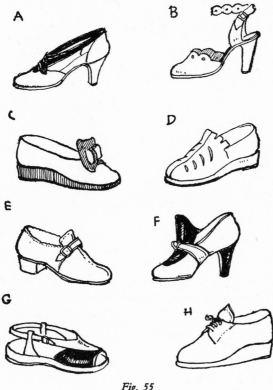

A

B

C

D

E

F

G

H

Fig. 55

Fig. 55 c and d for instance, might easily have been worn in the late sixteenth century, though their modern counterparts have naturally improved upon the original model.

Footwear

Figs. E and F are reminiscent of the seventeenth and eighteenth centuries, whilst G goes back into the ancient mists of early civilisation for its inspiration.

By 1938 the style and variety of shoes had reached a very high standard; the sizes and fittings obtainable then were more varied than they are today. To a great extent this was due to the American lead in producing "fashion" shoes and the growing awareness—because of the cinema —of the important effect that well-shod feet make on an ensemble. There is little doubt that the concept of the elegant world offered to the general public by the popular "society" film was influencing fashion quicker than any previous method of revealing the world to the world.

The ankle boot and zipper-fastened over-boot were worn in America many years before they were adopted by European countries. In America, where snow is a normal winter hazard, they had been a necessity; in England they were not really accepted until the second World War, when anyone who owned such useful articles was to be envied. Fleece-lined suede boots, or those made from sheepskin, were very expensive and had not been considered particularly useful; those who owned them were mostly people who indulged in winter sports. However, during the war years they became popular as an effective protective covering for the feet and ankles; they could be donned quickly and were suitable for both bad weather and emergencies.

For several years after World War II everything was hard to come by, particularly in England where rationing of clothes and shoes made any purchase a much-considered adventure, in which one was carefully weighed against the other as a necessary item of apparel; if a new pair of shoes were bought it might mean that there was no possibility of buying a much-needed raincoat or sweater. The restrictions of utility prevented any possibility of quick-changing fashions being considered, and shoes with durable qualities, solid construction, platform soles, or rather heavy medium-sized heels that would not be likely to get out of shape, continued to be worn well into the fifties. There were, of course, notable exceptions, and these were for the most part sandal-type dress shoes worn with the long evening gowns, which still continued their style of bouffante skirts with a backless or strapless top.

Slacks of all varieties had been adopted during the war years, but only flat slipper-type shoes or espadrilles or heavy walking shoes with a minimum of heel were worn with them. High heels were reserved for more formal occasions.

In 1947 Dior's "New Look" shook the fashion world. It heralded a new ideal in feminine dress and for many it was their earliest escape from the restricting uniforms of the services. As Dior's first collection of these new fashions was shown only a few months before the abandoning of clothes rationing, it was not long before the length of skirts descended with a rush; anyone still wearing a knee-length dress in the Summer of '48 was very old-fashioned indeed. This vogue in itself drew attention to the feet and ankles, and in a short time Italy stepped into the shoe market with elegant little sandals with a minimum of strap and an incredibly delicate high heel. (Fig. 56 A and B).

These heels were the forerunners of the stiletto heel, that bane of those who care about the beauty of their floors. The stiletto heel had left its mark in most of the Museums and fine houses of the world and had caused considerable damage to the floors of aeroplanes before anyone realised what was happening. In order to find a material strong enough to support the weight of the body on the almost pinpoint heel decreed by fashion, a metal support with a superficially covered end-tip had been introduced. Should the protective end-tip become dislodged, the heels became walking hammers driving nail heads into all floors on which they trod.

The pointed heel led to another fashion no less surprising, the arrow-point toe. By the end of the 50's it was difficult to find any sort of shoe that had not such a point. There were however some less exaggerated designs with the tip of the toe cut square and a small Louis heel, but the craze for narrow feet had set in and should anyone happen to have a wide foot the only answer was to buy French shoes.

The craze for pointed-toed shoes developed to such an absurdity that it became necessary for many people to wear shoes two sizes too large in order to accommodate their normal toes. The ultimate result was that the toes turned up, much as they do in a turkish slipper, and a fashion that had started as an elegant departure from a sensible utility style ended by making it seem that all women had very large feet. Especially was this noticeable during the phase when white shoes worn with dark stockings was the dernier cri.

Stiletto heels continued to penetrate floors, stick in gratings, snap off and generally cause annoyance until the

Fig. 56.—1960

advent of the gimmick shoes and boots which deluged the shops in the mid-sixties.

Footwear

From about 1964 boots became increasingly popular. Not because of their durability—as the late Victorians virtuously considered—but because by adding interest and emphasis to the knee and thigh they help to interrupt the

Fig. 57.—1966

elongated leg displayed by the mini-skirt. Every conceivable type has been reproduced during this period, designs from our own past as much as those from remote countries.

The Twentieth Century

Men's fashions include elastic-sided boots, the ankle boot, the Admiralty boot, cowboy boots and a dozen other varieties. Those for women are more varied in design and colour, as well as length, and Carnaby Street and Greenwich Village have displayed everything from pale mauve suede with holes cut in the sides and black patent leather decoration, lacing at the sides—to a plastic thigh boot that conveniently stretches so that there need be no fastening.

As the majority of these gimmick fashions are short-lived, these shoes are not made to wear well and they cannot reasonably be included in a progression of footwear. That we make use of old designs and those devised for other climates merely shows that such forms have their uses and can amuse the eye as decorative foot-coverings.

In recent years students have set fashions years before they have become obvious generally. As early as 1961, for instance, some girl students were wearing their hair quite long and ironing it, more or less in competition with other students who were experimenting with built-up arrangements copied from those of the wealthy woman with unlimited time (and money) to spend at her hairdresser's. In '62 they were already wearing boots, colourful and gay, and their young men were going to considerable trouble to acquire unusual boots of any description from junk shops, theatre wardrobes or friends who were lucky enough to have travelled abroad. Any boot was welcome as long as it looked different. Those who could obtain cowboy boots were well ahead of their colleagues, for the American West with its strangely different climate

Footwear

Fig. 58.

and way of life had come to be thought of as a sort of "Never-Never Land."

There have been for many centuries certain types of footwear that have proved so useful that they have never changed, regardless of fashion or the introduction of ideas from other countries. Among these are the shoes which were made originally by hand, by people whose need was greater than their purse. Such shoes include the wooden clog still worn in Holland and Belgium, the gayly coloured knitted leg-covering with a stitched sole attached worn in the Balkan areas and northern Italy, (See Fig. 58), moccasins from the North American Indians, the shapeless skin boot of the Arctic, sandals from the deserts, the black felt slipper of the French peasant and a dozen other interesting varieties of foot-covering from all over the world. Russian boots and cowboy boots were originally worn by those who spent most of their lives in the saddle, and in the recent past they were thought a symbol of fine horsemanship. Now it is their decoration, varied and interesting, which has attracted a new and enthusiastic public who probably have never ridden a horse at all. Most of these types of footwear are now available to everyone; they can, in fact, be purchased almost anywhere and are worn by anyone who cares to look different from the mass.

APPENDIX

In the following pages there are several carefully measured drawings taken from existing shoes in various museums in England. These will give the reader some idea of the manner in which shoes were cut and shaped during the centuries covered by this book. I have endeavoured to show the more straight-forward styles peculiar to each century and in so doing indicate how they were fashioned. Naturally there were dozens of variations, for man's ingenuity is limitless in the creation of the strange and exotic, but the selection given here is fairly representative.

The Roman sandals are perhaps the most enchanting, and are unbelievably simple. As most of these have been preserved for centuries in the mud of the river Thames, their condition is fairly good. It is possible though to see that most of the men's sandals were completely worn out, with holes both in the centre of the heel and on the ball of the foot. Their measurements also prove that their wearers were on the whole rather large men, 11½" being fairly usual from toe to heel.

These shoes were cut all in one piece, quite a delicate piece of cutting, as the straps had to be thin, but not too thin to bear the constant pulling of the thongs that tied them. The inside loops were normally much longer than those on the outside. Among these drawings I have included an unfinished sandal (Fig. 59) because this shows in the greatest detail just how these elegant little shoes were marked out and then cut from a flat piece of hide.

122

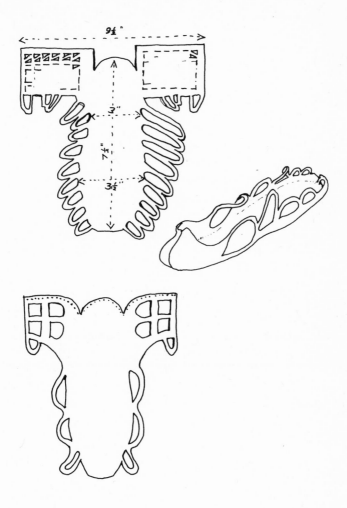

Fig. 59.

There were no seams except at the heel; had it ever been finished, the back part would have been all cut out in the trellis indicated. For how long into the Dark Ages such shoes were used nobody can tell, but their very simplicity must have had a long and continuing appeal to most workers in leather.

It is not until about the 13th century that we find a new type of shoe; but there are numerous pictures which indicate that such shoes must have been in use for some centuries. These early shoes are particularly interesting in that the sole was made with a seam under the instep; the reason for this seems to be twofold: first, for greater flexibility, and, second, to make it easier for the maker of the shoe to get at the inside when stitching. Shoes were often made at home and the very simplicity of the 13th and 14th century examples lend themselves to this, for they are very straight-forward and apparently needed no last. The inside of the leather supplied a sufficiently hairy texture through which to sew and the uppers were usually pierced so that they could be thonged together. From the 17th century to the present day shoes have been manufactured by expert specialists, with notable exceptions, such as the 19th century carpet slipper which was painstakingly embroidered at home and then taken to the local shoe-maker to sole.

Fig. 60 B2 shows an interesting example where the whole of the existing upper is cut in one piece, the piece from the top of the instep to the outside of the ankle is missing, but tiny stitch holes are visible on the edges that remain showing that once there had been a seam there.

124

This particular shoe (or boot), laced up the outside, apparently had some circular ornament let into the surface where the hole is indicated. The top is cut and punched as a decoration and was no doubt quite an elegant foot

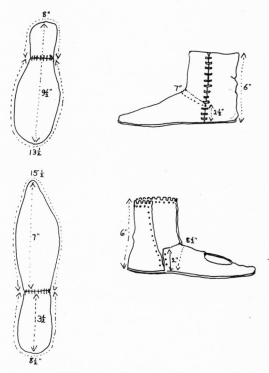

Fig. 60.—13th & 14th Century

covering in its time. The other example on the same page appears to be a lady's or boy's boot and in this case it laces up the inside (Fig. 60 A1 and A2).

Contrary to the usual ideas about Medieval shoes, these three examples are obviously made to fit the foot that wore them; the soles are quite definitely shaped for left foot

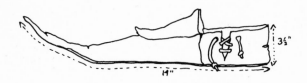

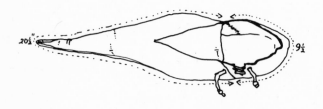

Fig. 61.—circa 1450

and right foot. Too, there never seems to have been any sort of seam at the back of the Medieval shoe until we get to the strange wide-toed shoes of the early Tudors.

Again one is struck by the simplicity and apparent clumsiness of what must have been a fashionable shoe. The top three drawings on this page are taken from one example which could have been lined with a contrasting

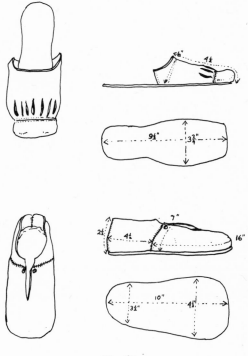

Fig. 62.

coloured material drawn out in puffs through the slashings across the toe, as was done in so many of the garments of this time. The heel covering is missing but a line of sewing holes remains to show us that originally this was a shoe and not a slipper.

Footwear

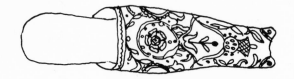

Fig. 63.—Early Seventeenth Century

By the end of the 16th century (see page 53) the shoe
had become something much heavier and the thick soles
had to be sewn or nailed onto the uppers. Elegant exceptions, of course, were the fabric shoes or slippers which
were worn for special occasions well into the 18th century.
One beautiful pair of fragile pink slippers finely embroidered in gold and silver thread with both the Tudor
rose and the thistle of Scotland is in the collection of the
London Museum (Fig. 63). The motifs suggest that these
quite possibly were once the property of James I. Another
pair of lady's slippers similar to those shown in Fig. 24
is also in the same collection (Fig. 64).

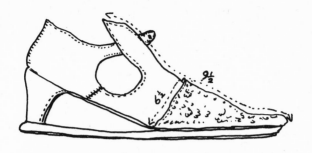

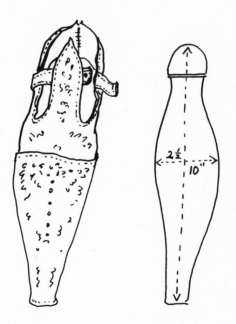

Fig. 64.—*circa* 1630

Footwear

Figure 65 shows the details of shoemaking at the end of the 17th century, the elongated toe is characteristic of nearly three-quarters of the century; the height of the heel normal after about 1660 though the shape of heels differed almost as much as they do on women's shoes today. The long narrow foot was the fashionable courtly shape from the Restoration until the Dutch fashions of King William.

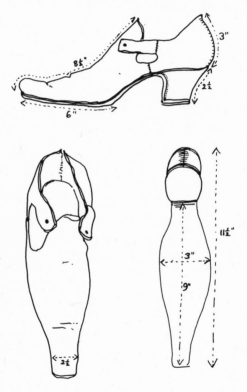

Fig. 65.—circa 1690

130

Appendix

Below are two varieties of 18th-century women's shoes. A shows the normal flaps attached to the side of the shoes which were fastened with a completely separate buckle (C). These shoes were made of brocaded silk with an embroidered rosette on the toe.

B is a leather example of a shoe that might have been worn almost anytime from 1700 to 1780, the flaps are made with an eyelet hole for a lace or ribbon and they were probably never intended to have any other fastening.

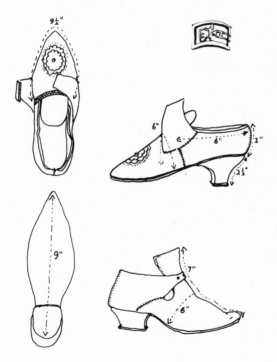

Fig. 66.—Eighteenth Century